AF481099

Bay County
A to Z

Written by **Lisa McLendon**
Illustrated by Olivia Clemons

ISBN 979-8-218-21402-9

Published June 2023

I would like to dedicate this book to:

My Family who are always my best cheerleaders

To my grandchildren who help make my world a better place
To Kerrie, Kim and Elyse for helping with locations

To all of the residents of Bay County, past and present, who have put so much back into the community and made it such a wonderful place to live

Lisa

~

To my niece, Katherine Jeanne. May everyday be an adventure in which you discover the splendor of every place you visit and of every person God places in your path.

To my family, whose love illuminated the beauty of life, and whose support has gifted me the opportunity to paint it.

Bay County's emerald green waters and white sandy beaches are truly beautiful, but its greatest beauty is the people who call it home.

I am grateful for you all.

Olivia

St. Andrew Bay is so big and deep
It hugs the city to earn it's keep
With massive ships either coming or going
The pass keeps everything smooth and flowing

The **B**ay Line Railroad has miles of track
That run from Bay County to Dothan and back
It brings lots of goods to the port and the town
Over 100 years old and still around

Coastal Systems Station is a big navy base
And the US Coast Guard is also in place
They train Navy divers to be best in recon
It's home to the hovercraft and Sea Dragon

In the water you'll see Dolphins galore
As they feed on the fish that swim close to shore
They like to jump and they like to race
And they always have a smile on their face

Econfina creek has a beauty that's rare
With rope swings on trees, if you so dare
It's a great place to go and bring a crew
To either tube, kayak or rent a canoe

Frank Brown Park is really cool
With a water park and a really big pool
Fields of soccer and baseball on which to play
Or enjoy a festival by night or by day

The Gulf is so wide and deep and blue
But sometimes has some green to its hue
Its fun to watch the waves rush to shore
And it's beauty makes you come back for more

The Hathaway bridge across the bay it spans
Gracefully connecting two pieces of land
At night it's lit with lights of blue
Walk it or drive it for a beautiful view

Shell Island can only be reached by boat
And once you get there you can swim or float
The gulf on one side, the other the bay
It's a wonderful way to enjoy the day

The Jetties are a line of rocks to view
To keep the pass open into water so blue
Dolphin and fish come to visit and play
Snorkeling is a great way to spend the day

Kayaks abound out in the bay
Paddling around and making their way
They glide through the water so it would seem
Some are yellow, some orange and some green

Lobsters have a party every year without pause
They have long spiny bodies but oddly no claws
They are ugly but delicious have no fear
As we celebrate them in October each year

The Martin Theater is a place you must go
As it's the only building dressed in art deco
It has plays and movies and musical feats
Come in and grab a comfortable seat

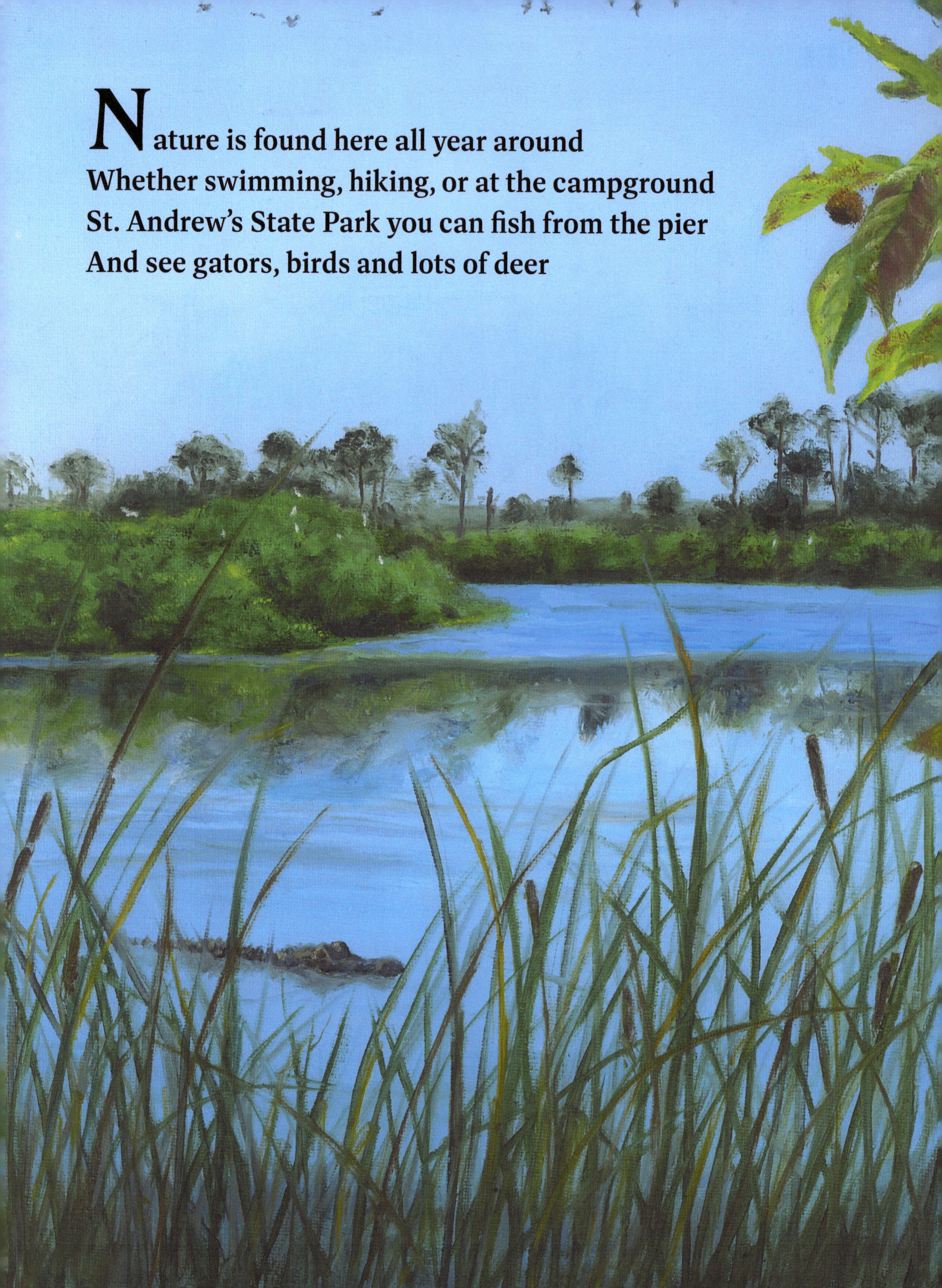

Nature is found here all year around
Whether swimming, hiking, or at the campground
St. Andrew's State Park you can fish from the pier
And see gators, birds and lots of deer

A 250 year old oak tree lives at Oaks by the Bay
A park just as pretty by night or by day
With a gazebo to sit and steps that reach
Down to the shore of the bay's sandy beach

A large red Pirate ship sets sail every day
Shooting its cannon out into the bay
In October the pirates all meet to fest
At the pier where the parade is truly the best

A Quest for fun,
it's worth the trip
Come on down
to the Miracle Strip
There's loads to do,
see and taste
So don't delay,
hurry, make haste

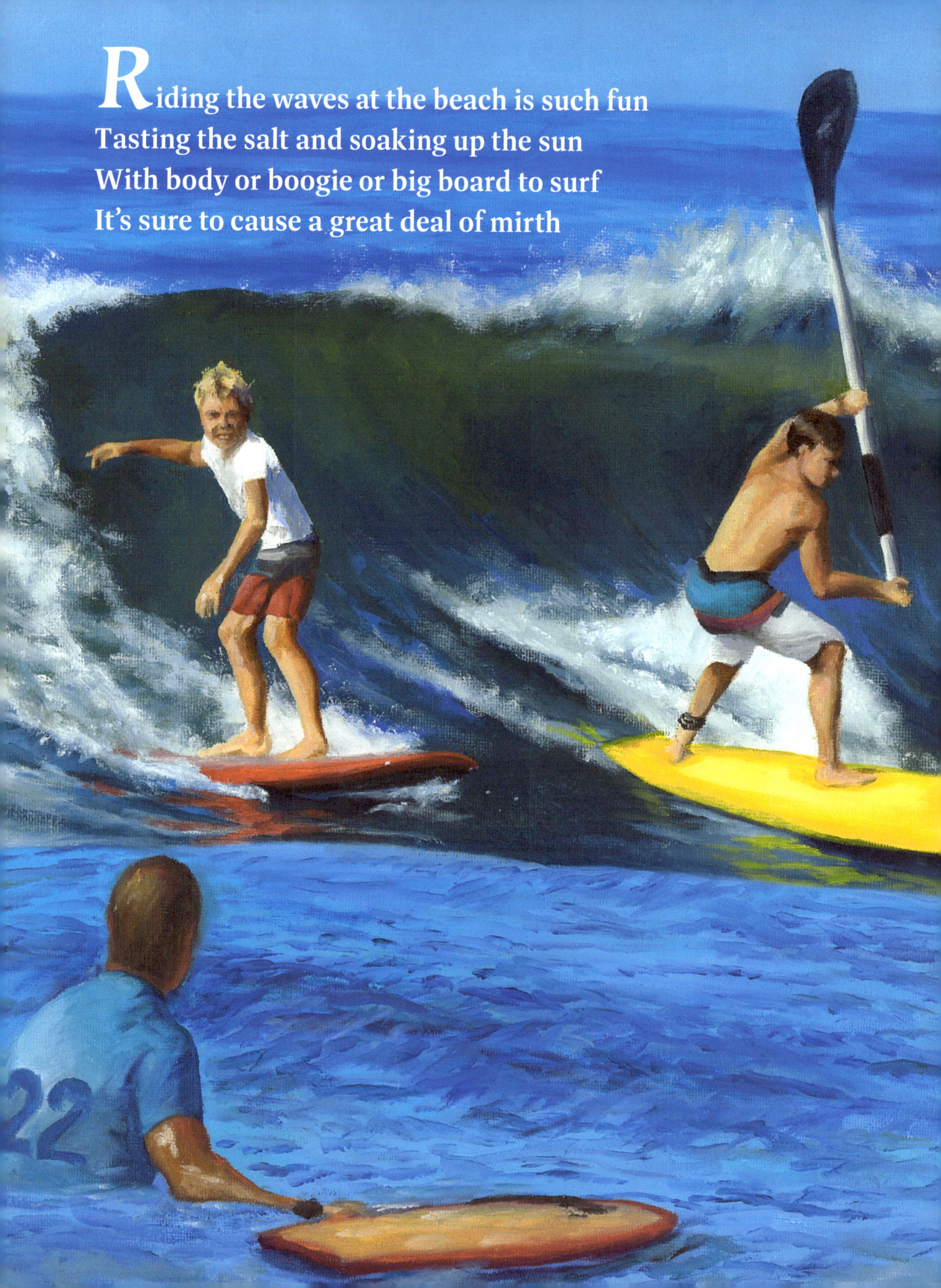

Riding the waves at the beach is such fun
Tasting the salt and soaking up the sun
With body or boogie or big board to surf
It's sure to cause a great deal of mirth

Sheffield Park
Is one of our most special places
They have music and festivals
Where they paint all our faces
There are farmers markets
Along with so much more
A library, too and a playground to explore.

At Tyndall there are drones and the world's fastest jets
When they soar through the air, it's as cool as it gets.
We're proud to be home to our heroes in flight.
They keep us all safe whether by day or by night

Under the Oaks Park sits on East Bay
There's a creative playground so come and play
It looks like a fort so bring a snack
Or take a lap on the walking track

Vacation is great in the county of Bay
Every day, come what may
Beaching or boating or ride a go-cart
You will leave a little piece of your heart

The **W**orld's most beautiful beaches are here
The sand is white and the water is clear
You can see dolphins and turtles and crabs galore
Play in the water or build castles on shore

X marks the spot for a ton of fun
In Bay County soaking up the sun
Lots to do and things to see
It really is a great place to be

A Yacht club will teach you how to sail
Whether the wind is flat or when it's a gale
Then tell your friends you know how to tack
So once you go out you can always come back

The **Z**oo is a place you want to be
To pretend that you are on safari
You can feed the goats with food you buy
But not the bears, tigers or snakes, oh my